Life-Changing Classics, Volume XXXIII

The Love of God

Charlie "Tremendous" Jones

Tremendous Leadership
PO Box 267 • Boiling Springs, PA 17007
(717) 701 - 8159 • (800) 233 - 2665
www.TremendousLeadership.com

ISBN-13 978-1-949033-50-2

Designed and Printed in the United States of America

Table of Contents

Introduction

by ***John Segal***

I first heard Charlie "Tremendous" Jones speak at a business conference in Atlanta. His short talk was so humorous that I decided to buy his recordings so I could steal the jokes for my own business talks. But doing so, I got more than I bargained for.

My family did not attend church when I was growing up. I had nothing but negative views of faith. However, between Charlie's jokes there was a clear and powerful message about the true character of Jesus Christ. I had never heard this before. I listened to the recordings 40 or 50 times and then, at Christmas, I called the number on the recording. Charlie answered the phone. My purpose was only to thank him for his message, but we made plans to meet and became lifelong friends. In our first meeting, Charlie guided me through scriptures opening the door to my life changing acceptance of Jesus as my Lord and Savior.

Charlie had a way of drawing you into deeper thoughts. His jokes had a twist to them, always with the purpose of blessing you with a clear understanding of Bible truth. He made complex things simple. He explained how God provides us with difficult life experiences, not to tear us down but to build us into the whole people He always intended us to be. I'm so thankful we have the opportunity to listen to these great messages of Charlie "Tremendous" Jones.

The Love of God

The Greatest Gift We Can Give Our Children

Years ago, I used to say, "The greatest gift a father can give his children is the memory that he loved their mother." I thought that sounded very good, and I repeated it for a long time. But a woman once said to me, "Mr. Jones, what if my husband left me?" I thought in response that she could still give her children a memory that she loved *him* and let them discover the truth about their father later in life. I felt it necessary not to rob them of the memory that she loved their father or that he loved their mother.

But then I understood this was not good enough either because I realized that there is something better. I said, "You know, the best thing is not giving them the memory that you loved their mother or their father. The best gift is the memory that you loved God." I continued to say that for a long time; it also sounded good. And yet, I recognized even further that I still had not gotten it correct. I realized that someday my children would find out that I was just like anybody else, that I did not love God—not like I should have loved Him.

Oswald Chambers makes a remarkable statement in his April 30th devotional in *My Utmost for His Highest*. He says, "If you try to prove to God how much you love him, that is a sure sign you don't love him." I began learning years ago that it is not that I love God, or that you love God, or that we love God. Instead, we are here to be learning how much He loves us. I hope you leave the memory to your children that while you may have loved God a little, you loved Him because He so loved us. We love Him because He first loved us, and we love Him back with the love with which He loved. Isn't that more wonderful?

Leave your children with a memory that you knew what it was to be loved by God.

Here is my life story: I'm not what I think I am; I'm not what I hoped I would be, nor what I ought to be—but, by the grace of God, I'm not what I was. I once was lost, but now I am found; I was blind, but now I see. That is my life story and I like to share it because that is your life story, too. That is the beautiful part about being a child of God; it's the same for all of us. Neither the pastor nor the evangelist receives anything more. Everyone gets the same Savior, the same love, the same forgiveness, the same acceptance, the same joy, and the same peace. Now you may say, "Well, how come he seems to enjoy it more than me?" You need to realize that that is your problem because you have all there is to have. The beautiful part about it is that every day you enjoy what you have, tomorrow you get to enjoy more of what you have. But if you are not enjoying what you have today, tomorrow you will enjoy it less, and soon you will be wondering if you have anything.

Don't Read Your Bible

Now I would like to invite you to ***think*** with me. Have you ever noticed what happens when people listen? They fall asleep! Not so when they ***think*** with you. This truth is so important. Let me illustrate it. Did you know it is sinful to ***read*** the Bible? **The most mixed-up people in the world read their Bible.** You might say, "You're kidding." No, I'm not. You should ***study*** your Bible. You should read your newspaper and study your Bible. Do not study your newspaper and read the Bible.

When you study the Bible, something incredible happens. You hide it in your heart. You do not need to memorize it as you study it. There are a lot of verses I haven't remembered but many I have. But I know many more verses than I ever memorized because of just studying the Bible. Over the years, some verses become a part of you, and you don't even recognize it. And that is why I tell you not to listen—because you listen merely with your ears. And if you hear too much, you get top-heavy in the head and too light in the heart!

The Bible tells us not to listen but to ***think*** on these things. Think, think. When you think, you begin to realize what you had memorized. And when you realize something, it will come out of you. When you only memorize something, you have to ***make*** yourself share it to show you know it. Realizing is different. You cannot contain that which you realize. Even if nobody listens, you still are compelled to share because in reality, you are not talking to them; you are thinking with them. And it would be best if you thought out loud to see how little you know about what you are saying. You may say to yourself, "Oh, that is really good. I'll rethink that again." That is why you should think about your prayers. You might pray something like, "Now, Lord, would you go with me?" After reflecting on this request, you realize that God must be thinking, "Why should I go with you? You can't get away from me." Why do we pray with such stupidity? Some people even say, "God, would you draw near me?" Well, He can't get any closer than in you! Why is it we do not thank God that He lives inside us?

Sometimes we say, "Lord, I'm so unworthy," and the Holy Spirit responds, "But I have counted you worthy; now quit moaning. Your unworthiness is why I chose you." So instead of praying to be made worthy, we should be thanking God that He has counted us worthy. Instead of claiming that we are not lovable, we should be thankful that we are accepted as His beloved and rejoice in this. This unconditional acceptance is the difference made manifest when we think and realize. We are accepted as His beloved. We are counted worthy. We are chosen, accepted, and loved. We need to cease asking for what God has already given.

Amazingly, as we think and realize these things, there is no need to try to witness. Trying to witness to others is like trying to love your wife. If you do not love your wife, quit trying— it gets worse! I will prove it. Suppose you are in bed and your wife says, "Sweetheart, I love you. Do you love me?" And you say, "I'm trying." What? You do not try to love. You are loved, and you respond with a love triggered in you that was once there yet lay dormant. That is why some people act like animals. Because they do not know what it is to be loved, they do not know what it is to be accepted, and they do not know what it is to belong. Thus, it is this word "love" that we are going to think about. Love.

Finding True Love

Many years ago, Prince Edward, the King of England and the Duke of Windsor, made a powerful decision. He gave up the throne of England to marry Wallis Simpson. The world said it was the love gesture of the century; they said that it was a demonstration of great love. I say that it was nothing. He was just head over heels in love. When someone is infatuated—that is not real love. Sure, we hear about all kinds of love affairs, but that is not real love. **Real love is something that goes beyond you. Real love is never that of being served; it is that of serving. Real love is always based upon this reality of giving of yourself, not getting for yourself.**

Early in my youth, I believed that there was no love. I had a mother and father like everybody else. My mother, being young and lovely and not able to accept the responsibility of having a lot of children in those Depression years, left us. As a young boy, I realized there was no such thing as real love. Some might say, "Well, there is such a thing as a mother's love." But for me and many others, we did not experience this. Our mothers or our fathers left us. Yet, I have to say that my mother was the most wonderful woman in the world. She is in Heaven now. Sin caused her to leave us. She did not mean to do it. She paid a terrible price for doing what she did.

When I came to know Christ, I immediately realized how wrong I was to be bitter about my mother leaving us. I never had to forgive her because God forgave me of my sins. She could never hurt me like I hurt my Savior. Over the years, I would call her on the phone. I bought her a home. I took her to Europe. And I told her every time we talked, "You're the most wonderful mother in all the world." And she was. But my point is that the love of Christ did that to me. Before I was loved by Christ, I did not feel this way. I wanted somebody to love me. **But no human being can love the way that God loves.**

No one can ever love anybody the way they need to be loved. No man can love a woman the way she needs to be loved. No woman can love a man the way he needs to be loved. That is why *John 3:16* is so critical. "For God so loved the world that He gave his only begotten Son." He gave Himself. If I would receive and believe in Him, I would never perish, but He would come into my heart and make me a new creature. I would be born again—not of the will of man but of God. Even after I went through the experience of my mother abandoning us as a young boy, I still had hope. You always have hope. We always have hope. And I thought, "Well, maybe there is no love in a person's childhood, but perhaps finding the right girl as a young man—maybe that would be it." And one day, I met the right girl, Gloria Burkhart. It sure was love at first sight! I did not rush her, though. I waited thirteen weeks before asking her to marry me!

I remember being so in love and on my best behavior. I did not want her to find out what I was like until I could get her married to me. Then she would help me become what I wanted to be. And I remember after thirteen weeks, I said, "Now, Gloria, I love you, and I want to marry you. But there are a few problems. I do not have any money. We cannot have a church wedding because I cannot afford it. I cannot give you a ring. You have to give—to loan me—$2 for the wedding license. And we have to borrow your father's car to sneak away and elope."

Her answer was yes! That showed how desperate she was. But I tell you, that was the greatest thing that ever happened in my life. She said "yes." "Yes!" And she believed in me. She was the first person in my life who believed in me, and she said she loved me. And not only that, she said she understood me. I just could not believe it!

Now, 50 years have gone by; I love her, and she loves me. But it never would have been a real love affair had not Christ come into my heart and taught me that I did not marry her for her to love me. He gave me to her to learn to love her even if she never loved me back. You never learn this truth from other humans or the world, but that is what drives you to Christ.

All of life is about discovering these beautiful truths. When we got married, I found very quickly that there were two kinds of love. First, please realize that we can say we love all we want. But there is one aspect of life that we all have in common. **No matter how rich or poor, or intellectual or ignorant, or young or old, or male or female, there is one need everybody has every moment of their life. That is to know they are loved and accepted and to hear these words in their heart, "I love you, and you know it, and you know how it is true."** While there was nothing Gloria could ever do that would ever make me give up or leave her, something still was not quite right. I believed that I was as close to real love as a person can get. But it was not enough.

Eternal Life Insurance

One day while I was out looking for somebody to sell insurance to, an old friend jumped into my car. He said, "Charlie Jones, how is it with your soul?" I asked him what he meant by this. He said, "Are you born again?" I had never heard the expression. He said, "Are you going to heaven when you die?" I said, "No one can know that. No one has ever come back; therefore, no one can know." And with that, he whipped out his little New Testament, and for the next 45 minutes, he made me read him verses. I had never met anybody like this. He did not tell me where to go to church; he did not tell me he was right; he did not tell me what to believe. He just made me read him verses. And they were beautiful verses. We read John 1:1 and John 1:12 and John 1:14 and John 3:3. We read the whole third chapter of John. Then, we read John 5:24, John 10:28, Romans 10:9-10, Ephesians 2:8-9, 2 Corinthians 5:17, and Romans 12:1. Verse after verse after verse. But when he had me read the final verse, "For God so loved the world," he told me to put my name in there so it read: "For God so loved Charlie Jones, that He gave His only begotten son, if Charlie Jones would believe in Him, he would never perish, but have everlasting life."

I said, "That's why I can't believe in God." He asked, "Why not?" "Because I would never believe in a God who would send anybody to hell." He said, "Read the next verse." The next verse said, "For God sent not His Son into the world to condemn the world, but that the world through Him might be saved. And he that believeth is not condemned, but he that believeth not is condemned already because he hath not believed in the name of the only begotten Son of God." **And I saw for the first time that God never condemned anybody; man's sin condemns him.** As for me, I had chosen sin. It was God who sent Christ in the form of flesh to die in my place that I might receive Him.

Some people say, "I'm giving my whole to God." Well, He isn't getting much then. Or one might say, "I'm giving my life to God." But you cannot give your life to Him; He gave you your life. And so that day when I received Christ as my Savior, it was because I had my first encounter with the greatest gift in all the world: ***the love of God in Jesus Christ.*** Now, some people say to me, "Oh Charlie, I wish I could feel God's love more." Well, then, it is only going to get worse for you because you cannot feel love. You know you are loved. I do not want to feel my wife's love; I want to know she loves me. What if her feelings change? I want to know that I am loved, whether she feels like it or not.

Knowing Love Versus Feeling Love

Remember when you asked your wife to marry you? Did you feel married then? No. Did you even feel married when you got her signed, sealed, and delivered? That is when you felt it, isn't it? Now, tell the truth. When the pastor said, "I now pronounce you man and wife," did you say, "I feel married!" No! You didn't ***feel*** anything. But if you had woken up in bed the next week and said, "Honey, I don't feel married anymore," she may have responded, "Well, you are, so you better not try to get out of it!" I have never felt married. On January 29th, 1948, I stood up, swore off every other girl in the world, and asked one little gal, Gloria Burkhart, to be my wife. And I became her husband. Over the years, I have been learning to become more of all of what I became that day. **And just like I have never felt married, I have never felt like a Christian.**

Just as on our wedding day I stood up and swore off every other girl in the world, in March of 1950, in my automobile parked on West King Street in Lancaster, Pennsylvania, according to the authority of the word of God, I bowed my head and in Jesus' name asked God to forgive me of my sins. He said He would. He also said He would come into my heart. He cleansed me from all unrighteousness and made me His son. Thank God I ***know*** that. Some people say that they wish they could feel the way I do. Well, I wish they could tell me how I feel because I do not ***feel*** anything. But I ***know*** that I am saved.

My dear friend, boldness does not come from our own act or initiative. It springs from the heart filled with the word of God and ***knowing*** that you are loved. Then one can speak as Paul did and say, "Give me praise or give me blame, whether hungry or full, I will thank You whatever happens." I will never be like Paul. I wish I could be like Paul, but I thank God that I have the same Savior as Paul.

I know I get a little bit disheartened with people and aggravated at times. Then I think of Acts 20:24 where Paul said, "But none of these things move me; nor do I count my life dear to myself, so that I may finish my race with joy, and the ministry which I received from the Lord Jesus, to testify to the gospel of the grace of God." **I realize that I get upset with people because I am not surrendered and submitted. I am counting my life**

as dear to myself. At these times, I need to ask for forgiveness from my Lord. "Lord, forgive me. I know who is guilty. I am guilty because I counted my life as dear to myself."

The Joy of Love

I have ***joy***. Paul says, "that I might finish my course with joy" (Acts 20:24). If it were happiness, then I would be unhappy because so many of my friends are unhappy. I would not feel comfortable being happy around all my unhappy friends. But I have joy. Again, I do not ***feel*** it. Jesus is my joy. Sometimes people say that they are losing their faith. I tell them that I am going to pray that they hurry up and lose it altogether. Because when they do, they'll end up with Jesus. Jesus is better than a person's faith. I am so glad that I do not have very much faith. Sometimes a man will say, "My faith is all that has seen me through." He has not been through much then. There will come a time in your life when you run out of everything—when you run out of hope, when you run out of faith, when you run out of love, when you run out of peace—and then you will be able to say with Paul, "Thank God, I have nothing but Christ and Him crucified." And that is my ambition—to know Him. And Paul could say that because Christ was all he had. He had the love of Christ, the greatest of all blessings.

And now I am so glad that I can love Gloria as I always was meant to love her. In addition, I have a greater joy than that of sharing my love with her. What brings the greatest joy is the knowledge that Jesus loves her. If your spouse does not yet know Jesus, by God's grace, that is just a matter of time. God's timing is different. But Jesus loves your spouse. My father-in-law did not get saved until he was 80 years old. He was always a wonderful, religious, moral man. He was a better man than I was, but he thought he would go to Heaven because he lived a good, religious life. Later, he realized that a person goes to Heaven because he has received the love of God and Jesus Christ. God so loved us that He gave his only begotten Son. **Remember; you cannot go to Heaven and say, "I am here because I love God." No, you are going to Heaven because He loves you. What a different story.**

A Love Letter from God

It all begins in Him. **If anyone says that they wish that they had more love, I tell them that they need to receive the gift of salvation.** It is then that they will receive all the love they are ever going to receive. Consider what happens in a love relationship. If two people in love have ever had to separate for a month or two due to travel or work, they probably wrote love letters. They may have talked on the phone. When Gloria and I got married, we had nothing. I knew I had to get some money. Back in the '40s, men were making a lot of money in Alaska, so I went to Alaska to earn an income. I wanted to be the husband that I needed to be. Gloria told me she was going to write to me every day. I thought, "Oh, brother! Wonderful! She is going to write to me every day! That is wonderful. If I cannot be with her, at least I will get a letter every day." But then she said she wanted ***me*** to write a letter to ***her*** every day. Now, who in the world ever heard of a man writing a love letter every day?

So, I used to write six or seven letters at once and drop one in the mail each day. She never knew. Now, though, I write every day. From my perspective, I sure did look for those love letters. I was down there at the post office waiting on them. And if I saw that the planes could not land, I did not feel so well. But on the other hand, when the weather was good, I knew that the plane was coming. I knew that there was going to be a love letter from Gloria Jones to Charlie Jones.

When I received those letters and I rushed back to the bunk, I would lie back in the hut, and I would read them. "My dearest Charles, I love you very much," they said. I would think, "I am glad because I sure love you, Gloria." "I wish you were home," the letter said. I wished I were home too. She signed it, "I miss you; I hope you miss me. Your loving Gloria." I would rush down to get another letter. "My dearest Charles," it said. "I love you very much." "Good," I thought. "I love you very much." "I miss you very much." "I miss you, too." "I wish you were home." Every day the letter said the same words, but it didn't matter to me. And if the plane could not land, I would get the old letters and read in-between the lines. I would find the juicy stuff I missed the first time.

The Bible is a series of love letters from our Heavenly Father. The Bible is personal to me and to you. We do not have to read the Bible to become saved. But when a person receives the gift of salvation, evidence of this gift and this faith is that of wanting to read the love letters from one's Heavenly Father who deeply loves him. If a person does not want these love letters, he would be wise to examine himself regarding genuine salvation. What else should we want to read? I love Chambers. I love Tozer. I love Watchman

Nee, Federline, and A.B. Simpson. I love them. But my friend, they are sinners like me. There is only One who loves me. There is only one name that is above every name. That wonderful name is Jesus. Someday, before this name, every knee shall bow, and every tongue shall confess. I love that verse. He lets me bow my knees this side of Heaven. I even bow my knees now. It is so personal. **But the word of God will not be enjoyable to a person if it is not yet personal.** It would be as if that person found himself reading a very personal letter intended for another person. At the least, it would not be enjoyable. It must become personal.

But I will tell you that when I read, "Therefore, if anyone is in Christ, he is a new creation; old things have passed away; behold, all things have become new" (2 Corinthians 5:17), I knew that verse was for me. That is what ***my*** Father said.

Further still, some will ask me if I am living a great life. My dear friend, Jesus said, "But as many as received Him, to them He gave the right to become children of God, to those who believe in His name" (John 1:12). That is meant for me also. And consider 2 Corinthians 2:14, "Now thanks be to God who always leads us in triumph in Christ, and through us diffuses the fragrance of His knowledge in every place."

Yet sometimes, we suffer. I think as the years have gone by that my heart aches more today than it has ever ached in my whole life. I have children and a granddaughter. There are heartaches. And I might have just sat right down here and cried my eyes out. But I have a love letter that says, "for the sufferings of these present times are not worthy to be compared to the glory that shall be revealed" (Romans 8:18). **And I also know that while I may have some heartaches and suffering, I am not suffering alone.** Imagine if I had to go through what I am going through without knowing that Jesus loves me; Jesus loves them, Jesus loves them more than I love them, and Jesus can do so much more than I could even ask or think.

And He won't do it in my time or the way I want it done, but He'll do it. Thank God I have confidence in somebody. But who would I have confidence in if I didn't have this word? These are the promises. Now, of course, we don't know all that the pastor or those who have put years into study know. We haven't been to seminary. I am just a plain Christian like you. But over the years—these 48 years of being a Christian for me—one accumulates verses. And when I was young in the faith, people were kind and considerate. They knew more than me. They let me keep on learning. And that is why we need to be kind and considerate too. We are to be patient and not interrupt or dismiss people. These love letters are from our Heavenly Father. And they allow us to grow.

God Can Use Anything

God uses writers from the past who have impacted us to impact others. For example, I know why people have invited me to spend time with them. I got a call last year, three times in one week, from Australia, and the gentleman said, "Mr. Jones, I had to talk to you." He said, "I think about you every day since you came to Australia for the first time in 1979. Every day, I think of you." I knew what he was going to say. He was going to say what they all say: "You got me reading Oswald Chambers." And he said, "Thank you so much." I could go on for an hour to tell you about people in England, people in Winnipeg, etc. But they all have had to experience Oswald Chambers for themselves.

And God uses suffering. People come into my office, and they come in all day long with all kinds of problems. Yet, in reality, I have more problems than they have. And that is the way it's supposed to be. God wants us to have some heartaches. **It is not that He wants**

to make our hearts ache, but He knows that the only way we will be dependent upon Him is when we have our backs to the wall. And we have to see how weak we are and that we are not strong like people think we are strong. **We only look strong because we are leaning on Him.**

Frankly, I am about the weakest man that I have ever met. And maybe I will get a little weaker so that someday I can be like Paul and say that I am the least of the apostles and the chief of sinners. Often people will come to see me and share that their spouse left them or share another significant problem. I open the November 5th devotional from Oswald Chambers with them. **Oswald Chambers shares here that if you are going to be used by God, He will take you through a multitude of experiences that are not meant for *you* at all. They are intended to *make you useful* in His hands.** And in so doing, you will never be surprised at what transpires in other people's lives. Then I see the tears come; I see their eyes light up. I am reminded of the tragedy and the heartache in my life since I was a boy. I recall the shame and humiliation I have been through, and I thank God for every suffering He gave me. "Thank you for breaking my heart, thank you for the rejection, thank you for the humiliation. Thank you that I was unloved, that I was unwanted..."

God has helped me to identify with all those people who feel unwanted and unloved. **Whatever happened in your life didn't happen for you. It happened so that God could make you sensitive to people around you.** Oswald Chambers never wrote a book. Yet here it is, the number one devotional in the world today—and he did not write it. He died in 1917 at age 43 of an acute appendectomy in Cairo, Egypt. His wife took all of his notes that she had taken on his outlined little talks. And she wrote. She lived long enough to write all these books from notes he left and things she wrote from things he said. So, I tell my wife, Gloria, "Honey, the world will never know how great a man I am. You haven't written down one lousy word I've said!" I am leaving her a lot of cassettes so that she can listen to me when I'm gone! I am just kidding. Gloria doesn't need to write down what I say because we have Oswald Chambers.

God gave us one Oswald Chambers. We don't need two. We don't need two Charles Spurgeons; we don't need two apostle Pauls. We don't need two of you; we don't need two of your pastor. We need just one! God made you that He might bring you to Himself, love you, and share His love letters with you. Whether you are feeling loved or you are feeling rejected and hurt, God is saying in your heart, "I love you." Now we perceive the love of God, how He did love us. Oh, how we are to love, to lay down our lives with our brethren. The Bible is just full of love, love, love, love. The book of 1 John in the 5th chapter is filled with this. What a wonderful reality it is to be loved by someone.

Jesus is Better than Usefulness

What is the heart of love? It is forgiveness. What is the most missing aspect today in almost every Christian's life? Forgiveness, forgiveness, forgiveness. My wife knows if she committed adultery once a year, once a month, it would kill me. But I would never leave her. The Bible says you can. I don't care what the Bible says in this respect. I would never leave her because she can never be as unfaithful to me as I am to God every day of my life. And if God won't give up on me, on what basis do I have of ever giving up on her? Forgiveness. I remember the person who broke my heart more than any other friend I ever had. I remember how bitter I was and how hurt I was. It took a few years, but oh, how I love him today. How I thank God that

He used him to break my heart, to teach me that those things I lost didn't matter. I would have never enjoyed Christ had I had those things.

My joy is not caused by my usefulness. It comes from knowing that He loves me. And thus, He can do whatever He wants. That is the essence of joy. It is wonderful to be used, but it is wonderful to enjoy Him and not be used. Sometimes if you get accustomed to being used, you want to be used. **But Jesus is better than usefulness. Just praising Him is what pleases Him the most.**

There is one more side of the love affair after the love letters: having children. I wonder how a wife would feel after becoming married if her husband said, "Honey, we're not having any children until we can afford them." Gloria and I could have never had any. "We're not having any children until we know how to raise them." How stupid can this be? I thought I was an authority on how to raise kids—until I had some.

Some say that God gives us children so that we can teach them. I believe it's the other way around. **God never gave me my children for me to teach them. He gave me to my children for them to teach me.** And thus, I say, "Alright kids, I can hardly wait for you to grow up and get some kids of your own so your kids can start teaching you what you are teaching me because so far this is pretty one-sided!"

Do you know what happens when my children break my heart? Do you know what God says to me? "They don't break your heart like you break my heart." I say, "Thank you, Lord, you're right again." No matter who hurts me, God says all day long, "Remember, Charlie, they don't hurt you as you hurt me." I respond, "That's right, Lord." **It is mighty easy to forgive people when you have been forgiven.** There is no effort at all. And that is what keeps some people from sharing the love of Christ. When I gave my heart to Christ that day in 1950, I went right home. I said, "Gloria, guess what happened?" She asked, "What?" I replied, "I accepted Christ." And she said, "That's nothing to joke about." I said, "It's no joke." And I quoted those two verses I memorized: John 3:16 and John 5:24. I knew John 3:16 from my childhood. But I quoted those two verses to her.

Now, I must say, for years, I did a lot of harm. I memorized chapters of the Bible to use for God. But then, after about 10 or 12 years, God began to change my response to the love letters in my heart from memorizing them, to quoting them, to realizing them, to enjoying them. And how wonderful it has been, as the years have gone by, to discover the Word.

Be a Witness

A man heard me speak in Atlanta, and he bought my cassettes to get some humor for a speech. He is the president of North American Products Corporation, the most prominent tool company in America. Ten years ago, on the day before Christmas, he called up and said, "Hi, we live in Georgia. I thought I would come and see you." I said that would be wonderful. He came in to see me, and we sat there at my desk. I proceeded like my friend had 48 years before, and I had him read scripture verses to me. He bowed his head and accepted Christ. His testimony ten years later is that God has used him to change a whole city. And I didn't say a word to him; all I did was plant the seed. One plants, the other waters, and God gives the increase.

So, my dear friend, God doesn't say you have to win souls to stay saved. God doesn't tell you to share your faith to get saved. He just says in the word, "Ye are my ambassadors, ye shall be my witnesses." A witness is not somebody who makes up something. A witness recounts what happens to them.

You don't need to take a course on how to be a soul-winner. **When the Lord opens a door, and you are enjoying Christ, all you do naturally is plant a seed.** It is a lot like going fishing.

All boys want to go fishing. I wanted to go fishing. But back in the Depression days, no one could afford any fishing tackle. Who in the world ever heard of buying a pole when we could hardly get enough money to eat, let alone buy a pole? I would get out an old tree limb, get some string lying around, and tie the string on this pole. Then I would find a rusty nail somewhere, I would bend the nail, I would hook that string onto the rusty nail, I would dig up a worm and drape the worm over the nail, and I would fish. Now, guess how many fish God made dumb enough to bite on a rusty nail. None. I never caught a fish. All those years I fished, I never caught one—but don't tell me I wasn't fishing. I was fishing; they just were not biting.

Similarly, I didn't see anybody getting saved. Yet God taught me, "You're not supposed to see them getting saved. That's none of your business. You are to be a witness. There are missionaries in Egypt who labored their whole lives without one convert. How dare you want confirmation and ask for a response?" This is the role of the Holy Spirit.

The Holy Spirit draws them; the Holy Spirit convicts them. You can get them saved, but they won't really be saved.

Conversion is when the heart sees a loss, and there is a cry out to God. If they don't know how to pray, you should help them pray, "Lord, help my unbelief. I don't know how to ask it." You then just guide them along a little bit until they get some scripture as a base upon which to learn, respond, and grow. I could tell you so many stories of God letting me watch as He converted people. Even now, it is more wonderful than ever just to sit there, watch them read to me, and watch them come to know Christ.

Rich in the Love of God

I want to share a story that I heard in 1951 at a convention. I borrowed money to go. We had nothing. But I just wanted to be there. I heard that there were many businessmen who knew Christ and manifested Christ living in them. I don't like to say that they were living for Christ because that's inaccurate. He was living in them. I will never forget. I got there, and I wanted to be the first one there. I wanted to get every blessing I could get. So, I arrived first on that opening night, and there was a big ballroom. In comes another man with an old suit and baggy pants and clodhopper shoes. He sat down next to me, and I, of course, said, "I'm Charlie Jones." He said, "I am R.G. LeTourneau." And I praised the Lord. This man did not know who I was, but everybody in America knew who R.G. LeTourneau was—he was a Christian philanthropist and well-known inventor of earthmoving machinery.

Westinghouse Electric Corporation paid him $3 million for his line of heavy equipment. That's a lot of money even now. Imagine 40 years ago somebody paying you $3 million not to compete with them for a year. He was a genius. But what made him different than any other man— than any other Christian before and since—was that he was against tithing. He believed that people should keep 10 percent and give 90 percent of all that they earned. Some say that is why God made him rich. But he went bankrupt a couple of times. It didn't matter, though, because he was rich in Christ.

R.G. LeTourneau told me a little story that day. He said, "Once, a little boy went to school for the first day, and he found out at school his mother was a tyrant. He found out she made him do twice as much work as all the other kids. So, he went home, got a piece of paper, and made out a bill for all of his services. The next morning when he went off to school, he put the bill on his plate. His mother came around to clean off the table, and she picked up the dishes and this piece of paper which said, 'A bill to my mother.' She wondered what was on his mind. The bill read: 'For going to the grocery store and getting the things you forgot to get on Friday: 5¢. For hanging up my clothes: 5¢. For cleaning up my room and helping clean off the dishes: 5¢. For saying yes sir, no sir, yes ma'am, pardon me, and excuse me: 50¢." And down at the bottom was the total: $1.35. Well, she thinks, 'I think I know how to fix this little scallywag.'

"So, she put $1.35 next to his plate and on the bill wrote, 'Paid in full, Mother.' The boy could not wait to get home. He had longed to see whether his mother had seen the light and was going to give him the money, or if he was going to be taken to the woodshed. Well, he could not believe it. He saw the money. The bill was lying there, as was the money. He couldn't wait to get back to school and tell the other kids, 'My mother's seen the light. Things are different around here now. I'm going to be paid what I'm worth!'

"Well, that night, he rushed home, gobbled down his supper, and noticed when he got up that there was a piece of paper under his plate. He picked it up, and he took it to his room. 'I will see what this writing says,' he thought. It said, 'A bill to my son from your mother.'

"Well, he never had a bill from his mother before, and he thought, 'I'll see what's on her mind.' Here is what he read: 'A bill to my son from your mother. For going through the valley of the shadow of death to bring you into the world: love. For rocking you to sleep when you were a baby: love. For pacing the floors and kissing away the tears and praying over you, never knowing whether you would live: love. For teaching you to walk and kissing away the black and blue marks: love. For cooking your meals and ironing your clothes: love. Love. Love. Love. Love. Love. Love. Paid in full. Love, Mother.' Well, he began to read over the bill a second time. Halfway down the page, he began to see how wrong he had been. His heart began to break. His eyes began to fill with tears. He laid down the bill from his mother, and he went and got the money. He went around to his mother.

"He said, 'Mom, here is your money back. You do not owe me anything. I owe you more than I can ever pay you. And I want to tell you I am sorry. And from now on, I want to do something for you—not because you pay me and not because you make me. I would like to do some things for you because

I love you. And I love you, Mother, because you so loved me.' "

Do you know why that story is fresh in my mind today, just like it was 47 years ago? That is my life every day. How many times I will say, or you will say, "Lord, how come I have to do so much and you do so little? Lord, if you'll give me this, I'll give you that. Lord, if you do this for me, I'll do that for you." And how we need to be like the little boy where we let God say, "Listen, my child, my beloved. I sent Jesus Christ to the valley of the shadow of death in your place. You can never be forsaken. Jesus hung on a cross. I was forsaken so that you can never say that you are forsaken. My Son, Jesus Christ, shed his precious blood, endured the cross, the shame, and the humiliation so that you would have a relationship with Me. He clothed you in My righteousness, and I will never leave you nor forsake you."

And every Sunday when we come to worship, every morning when we wake, every night before we go to sleep, we need to say, "Oh God, forgive me. Lord, forgive me for serving you because you bless me. Lord, even if you take back every blessing you ever gave me, I thank you for Jesus, my blesser. Thank you for being my Savior." And if you are a Christian, you need to say these words just like I need to say them. And if you are not a Christian today, you need to say, "Dear God, Lord, forgive me for keeping you out of my heart. I believe you in my head. But, Lord, love isn't any good unless it comes into your heart." **Loving with your head is no good. You need to let Christ love you in your heart, where you surrender and say, "Lord, I give up. I surrender."**

You don't need to *accept* the Lord. He has accepted you. All you do is yield the right of way. "Come into my heart, Lord Jesus." That is all you can do. That is love. Love. The love of God.

Read more excellent titles from our Life-Changing Classics Series available at TremendousLeadership.com

The 3 Therapies of Life (Charlie "Tremendous" Jones)

The 7 Golden Rules of Milton Hershey (Greg Rothman)

The 7 Leadership Virtues of Joan of Arc (Peter Darcy)

Acres of Diamonds (Russell H. Conwell)

Advantages of Poverty (Andrew Carnegie)

As a Man Thinketh (James Allen)

Books Are Tremendous (Charlie "Tremendous" Jones)

Bradford You're Fired! (William W. Woodbridge)

Breakthrough Speaking (Mark Sanborn)

Character Building (Booker T. Washington)

Discipleship (John M. Segal)

From Belfast to Narnia: The Life and Faith of C.S. Lewis (The C.S. Lewis Institute)

The Greatest Thing in the World (Henry Drummond)

The Key to Excellence (Charlie "Tremendous" Jones)

The Kingship of Self-Control (William George Jordan)

The Lincoln Ideals (edited by Charlie "Tremendous" Jones)

Luther on Leadership (Stephen J. Nichols)

Maxims of Life & Business (John Wanamaker)

A Message to Garcia (Elbert Hubbard)

My Conversion (Charles Spurgeon)

The Mystery of Self-Motivation (Charlie "Tremendous" Jones)

The New Common Denominator of Success (Albert E.N. Gray)

The Price of Leadership (Charlie "Tremendous" Jones)

The Reason Why (R. A. Laidlaw)

Ronald Wilson Reagan: The Great Communicator (Greg Rothman)

Self-Improvement through Public Speaking (Orison Swett Marden)

The Science of Getting Rich (Abridged) (Wallace D. Wattles)

Succeeding With What You Have (Charles Schwab)

That Something (William W. Woodbridge)

The Three Decisions (Charlie "Tremendous" Jones)

Walt Disney: Dreams Really Do Come True! (Jason Liller)

The Wit and Wisdom of General George S. Patton (compiled by Charlie "Tremendous" Jones)